READING A NOVEL

Books By Walter Allen

NOVELS

Innocence Is Drowned

Blind Man's Ditch

Living Space

Rogue Elephant

Dead Man Over All

CRITICISM

Arnold Bennett

The English Novel

Reading a Novel

TOPOGRAPHY

The Black Country

CHILDREN

The Festive Baked-Potato Cart

Six Great Novelists

ANTHOLOGY

Writers on Writing

Reading a Novel

WALTER ALLEN

PHOENIX HOUSE LTD
LONDON

Printed in Great Britain by
Staples Printers Ltd., Rochester, Kent, for
Phoenix House Ltd, 38 William IV Street,
Charing Cross, W.C.2.

First published 1949
Revised edition 1956

CONTENTS

I

Good Novels and Merchandise

ON JANUARY 2, 1886, Robert Louis Stevenson wrote a letter to Edmund Gosse. 'Let us tell each other', he said, 'sad stories of the bestiality of the beast whom we feed.' Reader, Stevenson meant *you*. And he goes on to say: 'What the public likes is work (of any kind) a little loosely executed; so long as it is a little wordy, a little slack, a little dim and knotless, the dear public likes it; it should (if possible) be a little dull into the bargain. I know that good work sometimes hits; but, with my hand on my heart, I think it is by an accident. And I know also that good work must succeed at last; but that is not the doing of the public; they are only shamed into silence or affectation. I do not write for the public; I do write for money, a nobler deity; and most of all for myself, not perhaps any more noble, but both more intelligent and nearer home.' To those words of Stevenson's every serious writer since his day will say 'Hear! hear!' And the nearer we come to our own time, the more heart-felt the applause will be. For every writer knows that he puts pen to paper at the risk of continual misunderstanding on the part of the majority of his readers.

During the nineteenth century, indeed from the beginning of the Industrial Revolution onward, earnest working men throughout Great Britain devoted their scanty leisure, their evenings and especially their Sunday mornings, to learning how to read and write, partly because they saw education as the key to material benefit, but also because, full as they were of religious or political zeal, they knew that they could not satisfactorily pursue their interests until they could read; they knew that they were just as effectively disenfranchised by ignorance as by lack of the vote. Well, since 1870, everyone in England not mentally deficient can, in theory, read and write. I say 'in theory' because call-ups for the services during the war showed that a much greater percentage of the population than was ever suspected cannot in fact read, is illiterate in the strict sense of the word, has never learnt to read at school or has forgotten how to do so within a very few years of leaving.

But if the experiences of the Army disclosed a substratum of absolute illiteracy among our supposedly literate population, one would expect that of those who could read a considerable proportion would be able to read only poorly, at a low level of understanding. And this is of course a fact. Despite the progressive increase in recent years in the membership of our public libraries, it is still largely true that the majority of the adult population does not read a book, much less buys one, from one year's end to the other. It gets along very nicely, thank you, without books; it has the Sunday newspapers, weekly magazines, the films, the Light Programme of the BBC. Yet it is my purpose to try to persuade you that reading is an art and therefore something worth practising and taking seriously! Why, you will ask, need we bother about the illiterates and semi-illiterates in our midst? Why can't we simply leave them to their innocent devices and read quietly by ourselves as best we can?

The answer is, the presence of this huge mass of illiterates and semi-illiterates—and here let me say emphatically that they are not confined to any one class—has an ever-increasing tendency to drag down standards of taste. It is for this mass that the purveyors of popular entertainment, film-makers and BBC alike, newspaper proprietors and owners of weekly periodicals, largely cater. Its existence shapes the quality of popular entertainment, just as in turn the quality of popular entertainment conditions the mass: a vicious circle. And the result has been a rift in our culture. Disraeli called England 'the two nations', meaning by that the existence side by side of the few rich and the many poor. England is still two nations, but now it is composed of the two nations of the culturally rich and the culturally poverty-stricken.

This schism is now officially recognized; in the organization of British radio we have, besides the Home Service, on the one hand the Light Programme, which largely consists of snippets of entertainment for the culturally poverty-stricken, and on the other the Third Programme, designed for the culturally rich. The Victorian artisan who had learnt to read at Sunday Early Morning School read precisely the same books, the same religious and economic works, the same novels and poetry, as the formally educated did; he would have been indignant if you had tried to fob him off with anything else. He aspired, as it were, to the Third Programme; he had not yet fallen a victim to the modern heresy—where standards of taste are concerned the most corrupting of heresies—that because a majority of the population likes and approves of a work that work is automatically good and valuable. He had not been taught the difference between lowbrow and highbrow, which is one way of indicating the split in our culture, and if he had heard of the difference he wouldn't have thanked you for calling him a lowbrow; he would have resented any comparison between the structure of his forehead and that of the anthropoid apes.

But now anyone who dissents from the dangerous view that what the majority likes is automatically good and valuable, is immediately called a highbrow, or a culture-snob, or precious. Take, for instance, the following extract from a leading article on the work of the BBC; it appeared in a provincial evening newspaper:

> ... If the Third is to reach a vast new body of listeners it will have to cut out much that is far too precious. Why play to the wilderness? The Third's listening figures are falling, and culture-snobbery is the reason. In music the Third is certainly first-class, but in other items it lacks the light touch. Sir William Haley ought to flutter the dove-coteries and let in daylight from the real world.
>
> That is the course Wilfred Pickles has pursued and why he is No. 1 radio favourite. 'Have a Go' plays to twenty million people in its three weekly broadcasts. It succeeds on its sheer humanism. It puts every man in his own good humour and confidences that are often of absorbing social significance.
>
> Pickles's endless serial has even ousted 'Itma' from first place, but

there again the lesson is plain. The undertones of life blend with the Handley fantasia. Third on the list comes Twenty Questions, typifying the parlour game spirit which appeals to the Clever Dick that lurks in all of us. The Third, if it is not to be supercilious, can learn something from all these.

The inferences of the article are interesting. What appeals to twenty million people is automatically more valuable, *better*, than what appeals to half a million (which is roughly the listening figure for the Third Programme), and what appeals only to half a million is automatically precious and the result of culture-snobbery. And there's another inference: that what is good ought to be immediately accessible to the huge majority whether it has been trained to receive it or not.

Translate that into terms of literature. The greatest long poem in the English language is *Paradise Lost*; the greatest poem of our time in the English language is T. S. Eliot's *The Waste Land*. They are both very difficult poems; they demand, quite apart from a high degree of literary taste and sensibility in the reader, a wide knowledge of other poetry in several languages. Judged by the standards by which the *Yorkshire Evening Post's* leader-writer judges the current output of the BBC they are worthless, so small is the number of people in relation to the whole population that can enjoy them. Anyone who does enjoy them is obviously a culture-snob. . . . A century ago, even fifty years ago, the leader-writer's test would have been laughed at as absurd; the notion that what pleases the illiterate and the ignorant is therefore better than what pleases the educated and the trained would have seemed too ridiculous to admit of argument. Today, I may confidently expect someone to say to me: 'You say *Paradise Lost* and *The Waste Land* are great poems and you admit that for the great majority of people they are meaningless. How can they be great? You're a reactionary; probably a fascist. Justify yourself.'

I shall not try to do so, any more than I should try to explain the greatness of Mozart's chamber music to a man who was tone-deaf or the superiority of Rubens over a tinted photograph to someone who was colour-blind. I will merely say this. The merit of a book has nothing, nothing at all, to do with the number of people who read it. Its reputation is made by what Arnold Bennett used to call the 'passionate few . . . who enjoy literature as some men enjoy beer'. Their number is small, a few thousands, not more. Theirs is as much a gift as the ability to pick winners is, or, to go back to Bennett's analogy, the ability which really knowledgeable beer-drinkers have of being able to tell, even though blindfold, what part of the country they are in merely by tasting the local brew. I say it's a gift, for the real reader, like the real poet, is born, not made. But even the poet's gift is nothing without constant practice and exercise; and that is even more true of the reader's. And by constant practice and the exercise of one or two virtues, the nature of which will soon become apparent, it is not difficult for a reader, even though he lacks the gift which is the prerogative of the passionate few, so to sharpen his faculties as enormously to increase the value of his reading. The first essential is goodwill.

2

Why Read Novels?

GOODWILL to whom? Goodwill to the author of the book being read. But before we can discuss what that implies we must first of all decide why we read at all.

Plainly there are many reasons for reading. I have just moved to a house in the country. The garden has been neglected for years. The apple-trees are overgrown, have been allowed to run wild. Knowing nothing about the care of fruit-trees, I have bought a book on the subject. One reason for reading, then, is simply to get information. But this is merely one reason. When my wireless set goes wrong, for instance, I don't buy a book to find out how to repair it. It's easier and quicker to call in a radio-mechanic. There isn't time in life to learn everything about the thousand and one things that can go wrong. So this kind of reading, reading for essentially practical purposes, is not the subject of this essay.

Then, of course, everyone who reads at all reads on occasion to kill time. In certain moods some of us, if we have nothing else to read, will make do with the telephone directory or a railway time-table. This purposeless consumption of reading matter needs no defence but is equally not the subject of my essay. But it is important to it because reading for the sake of distraction is probably the main way in which many people come to reading, or to the reading of books as distinct from newspapers and magazines. This the war showed, when thousands of people, bored in barracks or in air-raid shelters, began to read books for the first time. Some went on to become genuine readers; some remained as aimless as they began. They read to be taken out of themselves, as they say. In a sense that is what we all do. What is important is where we allow ourselves to be taken.

It is not my purpose at all to be superior at the expense of those people whose reading consists only of what we call 'escapist' literature, what used to be called servant-girls' romances, though in fact they are read quite as often by middle-class women as by servant girls. Such romances, which are the literary equivalents of the great bulk of the world's film output, satisfy a psychological need in their readers; their existence is an index of the frustrations that attend the desires of so many people in the modern world. But at the same time they do not fall within the scope of my argument, for they are not books in the sense in which I am using the word. They are, like most films and most radio programmes, simply consumers' goods, marketable commodities, made to a formula to meet a demand. They bear the same relation to real books as advertisements bear to poetry. They are bad only in so far as they persuade their readers to prefer a dream-world to the world of life itself and in as much as continued reading of them enervates their reader's will in the face of life. But I might as well say straight out that people whose object in reading is to escape the problems of life may close this little book forthwith, for the subject-matter of real books is, quite simply, life in all its aspects, its mysteries, its ardours, its endurances, its problems.

Dr Johnson in his novel *Rasselas* speaks in a tremendous phrase of 'that hunger of the imagination which preys incessantly upon life'. It is precisely out of that enduring aspect of the mind of man that real reading like real writing springs. We read out of our everlasting curiosity in the enigmatic face of life, and this is true whether we are reading philosophy, records of religious experience, scientific research, history, biography, poetry or fiction, all of which are manifestations of man's experience of life and his abiding curiosity concerning it.

But let us narrow down our inquiry a little. In this essay I shall be concerned mainly with the reading of novels, because it is the novel which is the most important vehicle of imaginative writing in our time. I shall not attempt to define the novel, for where everyone else has failed it is improbable that I would succeed. I am going to assume that novels are mainly about people. Why do we read them? For several reasons, of course. Fundamental to them all is the sheer, naïve, age-old delight in the story, in wanting to know what happens next in a chain of events. Primarily we read novels for the same reason as we go to the pictures or watch a play, to be entertained, to be diverted. Entertainment, it need hardly be pointed out, can range from having one's ribs tickled to being purged by pity and terror, but unless the reader is entertained, all else fails; and the basis of entertainment in the novel is ultimately the story, what-happens-next. After that, we read because we want to know about the characters who set the events in motion, to whom the events happen.

We are all of us, since we are human beings, interested, absorbed in, human nature; but in the ordinary traffic of living we can know few other human beings with anything like intimacy. Still less can we fully understand them or their behaviour. Indeed, it is rare that we really understand ourselves. Fiction offers us the opportunity of knowing representations of human beings with a far greater intimacy than we can ever know actual human beings; and so much is this true that there are many characters in the world's fiction which are in a sense more 'real' to us, more comprehensible, than all but one or two of all the living people we know personally. So the novel ministers to our passion to understand our fellows; indeed it is in this age its principal expression. In good fiction (as of course in good poetry and good plays) we may find what Bernard Shaw found in the drama of Ibsen when it was first introduced to a comatose, all but moribund English stage in the eighteen-eighties: 'stories of lives, discussion of conduct, unveiling of motives, conflict of characters in talk, laying bare of souls, discovery of pitfalls—in short, *illumination*'—the italics are Mr Shaw's—'of life'.

But the reader cannot expect to receive illumination of life from a novel without some effort, without a willingness to adjust his mind to that of the author of the novel. Real reading, reading that is a creative act, is achieved only when there is collaboration between the reader and the novelist. And the novelist's part in the collaboration has already been done, or should have been done, when the reader takes up the novel to begin to read.

How can the reader collaborate with the author? That is the theme of this essay.

3

The Classic and Contemporary Fiction

BUT AT this point it is necessary to digress. My readers are protesting. 'You talk', they complain, 'of fiction, of novels, of illumination of life. The classic novels may give illumination of life; we'll take your word for that. But what about contemporary novels? Are not many or most of them worthless? We're busy people; our time for reading is limited; we don't want to read through a heap of worthless fiction on the off-chance of receiving illumination of life from one in a thousand.'

Of course you don't; and of course the majority of books that are published and sold as novels are worthless as literature. In 1948 no fewer than 1,831 new works of fiction were published in Great Britain alone. A considerable number of these were detective novels and thrillers; some were Westerns; probably the majority were written to cater for the day-dreams of women with either too much to do or too little. This glut of fiction is one of the main difficulties in writing about the contemporary novel. We need a word to distinguish between the market commodity, the novel written and published as consumers' goods, and the novel which was intended, at any rate by the author, as a work of art. It is this latter kind of novel, the novel proper, which I am dealing with here. Perhaps a hundred of them were published in 1948. Most of them could be read with pleasure in 1948 itself; perhaps twenty of them will be interesting to read in twenty years' time; it will be remarkable if half that number will be read, except by scholars, in a hundred years' time. Obviously the reader new to fiction would be quite rudderless if put down in a bookshop or library and told to choose out of the year's output of fiction those which offer illumination of life. But no one need be in such a position.

Every week the new novels are sifted and reported upon by the reviewers in the newspapers and periodicals. Reviewers are often attacked; by authors, publishers and public alike; and, of course, there are good reviewers and bad. But the reader who tried to select among the mass of new fiction without first consulting the reviewers would be in almost as hopeless a state as a sailor who set out to sea without benefit of Admiralty charts and the Nautical Almanac. The reviewer's job is to read a novel, find out what the author has set out to do, estimate how far he has succeeded, decide whether his intentions were worth while, and report his conclusions to his readers. The job is not so simple as it sounds. The value of a reviewer depends entirely on the taste, knowledge of literature and of the novel in particular, experience of life, enthusiasm and sincerity which he brings to bear on the book he is reviewing. Reviewers possess these qualifications in varying degrees, and the reader must discover for himself the reviewers who seem to him most trustworthy. This is not especially difficult. The more important papers which regularly print reviews of current novels include *The Times Literary Supplement*, *The New Statesman*, *The Spectator*, *Time and Tide*, *Tribune*, *The Listener*, the *Daily Mail*, *News Chronicle*, *Manchester Guardian*, *Observer*, *Sunday Times*, the *Daily Express*, the *Tatler* and *Illustrated London News*.

After following the fiction reviews in any one of these papers for a short time the reader will realize that not all publishers who publish fiction publish novels that are likely to afford illumination of life, that in fact the number of publishers who publish good novels as a policy and not by accident is probably not more than a score, and of these a handful are likely to publish better novels, *as a regular thing*, than the others. The publisher's name on the spine of a novel is itself, then, a good rough-and-ready guide to its level of quality.

But here the reader interrupts again. 'I've tried following the reviewers, and it's very bewildering. Why, only the other week the reviewers in the *Sunday* —— and the *Daily* ——said that *Blood for Supper*, which the publishers claim has already sold half a million copies in the United States, was a masterpiece, a work of genius, while the reviewers in the literary weeklies said it was pretentious nonsense. Who am I to believe? And what kind of guidance is this when reviewers often disagree about the merits of the same novel?'

Of course it is true that reviewers often disagree among themselves on the merits of particular novels. As suggested above, this may be due to differences in levels of taste and knowledge of the reviewers in question; but it is not rare for two reviewers of comparable status and authority to differ violently about the same book. And this is not at all strange. A great French novelist defined literature as 'life seen through a temperament', and a man's approach to literature is plainly conditioned by his temperament. This means that when estimating the value of a reviewer his temperamental idiosyncrasies must be taken into account.

'But,' the reader may ask, 'would I not do better to confine my reading in fiction to the novels of the past, the classic works? Their value is guaranteed. I'll know that I won't be wasting my time on the ephemeral.'

The answer to this is that the reader who confines his attention to the fiction of the past misses almost as much as the reader—much more common, no doubt—who reads nothing but contemporary fiction. For the question suggests that the fiction of the past, the classics, are somehow fixed and static. This is not so. All reading, whether in the past or the present, is a voyage of discovery on the part of the reader. It may be true that contemporary novels often seem thin and lightweight when read side by side with the masterpieces that time, which means nothing more or less than successive generations of Bennett's 'intelligent few', has sifted from the world's output of novels; but it is also true that our appreciation of both classic and contemporary novels can be heightened if both are read judiciously and impartially.

Needless to say, any estimate of a modern novel is valueless unless it is based on knowledge of the great work of the past; but at the same time our estimates of the great work of the past are always being altered, however slightly, in the light of the novels of the present. For, in fact, all literature, both of the past and of today, exists as it were in an eternal present. We speak of the tradition of the novel, but tradition is not a dead thing, the classics, not so many books behind the glass of the Victorian book-case. Tradition is a living force, which grows and changes as it takes in more and more work of the present and the near-present.

To take a concrete instance: James Joyce's great novel *Ulysses* has altered our whole conception of the novel; which means that as a result of that book we can no longer see classic novels like Fielding's *Tom Jones* or George Eliot's *Middlemarch* in quite the same way as readers did before James Joyce wrote. So every new novel which is good and not merely a repetition of a novel of the past (which is what popular, best-selling novels frequently are) modifies the tradition of the novel. There may often be dissension among reviewers about new novels, for no novel can be adequately judged until it is seen in perspective, which is scarcely possible at the time it is written. The reviewer's judgments are not absolute; in the case of work that is new, vital, of literary merit, his judgment can only be tentative. But—and this is the important thing—fundamentally the same kind of assessment of new books which the reviewer undertakes is constantly being made of the great works of the past. The classics, even the very greatest of them, are continually coming up before the judgment of the 'passionate few'. In literature there are no final verdicts. We do not see Dickens in at all the same way that our grandfathers saw him, and we see Thackeray and Trollope, for instance, very differently indeed from them. The special preoccupations of an age lead it to works of the past which the preceding age, with its different preoccupations, neglected or ignored.

There is today, for instance, a revival of interest in George Eliot and Henry James which would have astonished people even twenty years ago. Such revivals of interest in certain works of the past are not casual; they are intimately linked with the writing of the age itself, for, like the writing, they are manifestations of the age. Matthew Arnold said of Shakespeare in a famous sonnet, 'Others abide our question: thou art free.' He was wrong: not even Shakespeare is free. A classic is not something static; it may not even be permanent. Read Sir Walter Scott's *Lives of the Novelists*. It contains, as one would expect from so great a practitioner of the art of fiction, much fine criticism; but at least five of the fourteen novelists he writes about, novelists who were important in his day, are now forgotten except by literary historians.

There is another reason why we should not neglect or scorn contemporary fiction. The best imaginative literature at any time represents, as perhaps nothing else can, the growing points of its age. In the literature of an age its conflicts, tendencies, obsessions are uncovered and made manifest; to a degree which is continually astonishing, good writers are, so to speak, mediumistic to the deeper stirrings of the life of their time while they are still unknown to, or at any rate unsuspected by, the public, politicians and current received opinion. The classic novels make the past familiar to us: that is one reason why we read them. But since we are living in the present, immersed in it, it is exceedingly likely that we do not recognize its real nature, any more than we can see ourselves except in a mirror. Contemporary novels are the mirror of the age, but a very special kind of mirror, a mirror that reflects not merely the external features of the age but also its inner face, its nervous system, the coursing of its blood and the unconscious promptings and conflicts which sway it.

And then we must remember that there was a time when the classic novels themselves were new, when men reviewed, discussed, and talked about Fielding and Scott and Flaubert as we today review, discuss and talk about Joyce Cary and Graham Greene and François Mauriac. The classic novels survived their publication and endured because the passionate few of their day cared seriously about them. If the passionate few of the present confined their attention only to the work of the past then literature would die. There would be no more future classics. So the reader who cares for literature has a special duty towards modern literature, the duty, no less, of keeping it alive; the duty, at least, of seeing the conditions for its survival continue.

The best way to read fiction is to mix one's reading, neither to favour the present at the expense of the past nor to favour the past at the expense of the present. And do not think that if this policy is pursued, contemporary work will appear thin and trivial beside the great work of the past. It is not necessarily so at all. As a professional reader I have to try to keep abreast with contemporary fiction while constantly widening and deepening my knowledge of the fiction of earlier times. I am continually turning from the most vital work of our own time to the classic novels and I find no opposition between them; they are not mutually exclusive. Why should they be? Dickens and Tolstoy and Jane Austen were concerned ultimately with the same task and the same problems as Joyce Cary and André Malraux and Elizabeth Bowen: they are all working, as it were, at the coal-face of the same mine. I have vivid recollections of reading James Hanley's novel *No Directions* in the intervals of re-reading Dostoevsky's *The Possessed*, probably the most powerful novel ever written. James Hanley is one of the most interesting of contemporary novelists; he is also one of the most uneven. I would not say that *No Directions* successfully fulfilled Hanley's intentions in writing it. It ought, therefore, one might have thought, to have been quite overwhelmed by *The Possessed.* I did not find it so. I found that Hanley and Dostoevsky, however different their stature, were fellow-artists united in integrity and in a common passion for recording the truth as they saw it. They had both been to the same well; that Hanley's bucket was so much smaller than Dostoevsky's didn't make the draught he brought from it the less welcome.

I am not, of course, suggesting that we should read contemporary novels with an eye to their becoming classics in a future time. That would be altogether too self-conscious a way of reading. It is obviously impossible to say categorically of any one new book that it will be read and enjoyed by posterity. The qualities that go to make a classic are not necessarily immediate at the time of publication. All one can say is that it is extremely unlikely that novels of the international best-seller class will have the enduring qualities which will lead to their being read with pleasure in a hundred years' time, or even in twenty. Thus, it is certain that *Forever Amber* will be unreadable even in ten years' time, and I cannot easily conceive *Gone with the Wind* being read by our children. On the other hand, I would not be at all surprised if L. P. Hartley's 'Eustace' trilogy, *The Shrimp and the Anemone*, *The Sixth Heaven* and *Eustace and Hilda*, was read with delight by our children's grandchildren. Mr Hartley's books were not tremendously successful in any financial sense. One would not call them 'great' novels. Were *Emma* or *Persuasion* called great on first publication? But it was obvious to the passionate few that they were well-nigh perfect.

Novels that are enormously popular on publication are so for much the same reason that certain dance tunes are enormously popular; because they are, as it were, easy to pick up. By the same token, they are just as easily forgotten; they are displaced by the next book that proves easy to pick up. This is not, of course, to deny that there have been international best-sellers possessing the survival value of classic novels. The work of Dickens is an obvious example. But it is very, very unlikely that the social conditions which could nourish a Dickens will recur within any foreseeable distance of time in Western Europe or America. So there is a moral: by all means read the international best-sellers if your curiosity prompts you to, but don't expect to find in them those qualities which are the source of illumination of life. You are much more likely to find them in the novels of men and women whose names not more than one person in a thousand will have heard of.

4

The Novelist's Obsession

So MUCH for that necessary digression. We were discussing, before we were led off the track of our argument, reading as an act of collaboration between reader and writer. I said that reading of that kind alone could be regarded as creative. But how is the reader to collaborate?

It is surely necessary first of all to be able to recognize the novelist's intentions. Thus, I once heard a young woman who had just 'read' *The Years* complain bitterly of Virginia Woolf's inability to create a solid, three-dimensional world; Mrs Woolf, she assured me, was 'not as good as Sinclair Lewis'. The very comparison between such wildly different (though in their individual ways good) novelists proved that she had failed to understand Mrs Woolf, even if she had succeeded in understanding Mr Lewis.

Let us see, if we can, why the novelist writes novels. One of the best contemporary novelists, Elizabeth Bowen, has defined the object of a novel as 'the non-poetic statement of a poetic truth'; one of the best contemporary poets, Louis MacNeice, has defined poetry as 'a precision instrument for recording a man's reaction to life'. The novel is a branch of poetry; it is the expression, in terms of characters and story, of what the novelist has discovered about life in the course of living it. The greater the novelist, the more profound will be the discoveries he makes and expresses in character and story. A good novel is always the revelation of the novelist's own self-discovery.

But why does the novelist, you may ask, express his discovery about life in terms of fiction? Why can he not tell us what he has found simply and directly, without plot and character, without the frills? Simply because he is a novelist; if he could dispense with plot and character he might be a philosopher or a psychologist or a sociologist, but he would not be a novelist. For plot and character are the language the novelist employs to express his discoveries about life. Indeed, it would be true to say that it is through his obsession with plot and character that he makes his discoveries, enshrines them in an image of life. Of course different novelists have different theories about their art; they write, they think, for all sorts of reasons: to reform the morals of the age, like Fielding; to expose current social evils, like Dickens; to make money, like Balzac; they frequently believe they are great reformers or deep thinkers. They may do all these things and be all these things; but *only incidentally*. Fundamental to everything else is the obsession to create through character and story, which can only artificially be separated, an image of life.

I say 'obsession' deliberately. For good novels are not so much written as force themselves to be written. Once conceived, a novel, like the foetus in the womb, grows with a life that is certainly nourished by the novelist but that is independent of him. And the conception itself of the novel is outside the novelist's conscious control. There are all the people in the world about him, all the drama of life on his doorstep: you would think, therefore, that the novelist could pick and choose his material, his characters and his theme. This is not so; the fructifying incidents, the sudden perceptions, that will impregnate his novelist's imagination belong to the individual novelist alone. That is why a good novelist is a man possessed.

In all this, where does the reader come in?

While the novel is being written, scarcely at all, I am afraid.

Remember Stevenson's words: 'I do not write for the public; I do write for money . . .; and most of all for myself.' D. H. Lawrence said much the same thing when he wrote, 'My motto is, "Art for *my* sake".' For a novel, while it is being written, is a personal discovery. Consideration for its readers comes much later; indeed, it may not come at all: there are instances of great novelists and poets who have cared so little for being read that they have not even bothered to get their work published in their lifetime.

'So', you will say, 'the novelist's attitude to his work and to the public is, "Take it or leave it?" ' And the answer must be, 'Yes; fundamentally, yes.' But it is my task to persuade the reader to take it and not leave it. That as a consequence of his writing a novel a reader is entertained, moved, amused, edified, may even have his life wholly changed, may be, as far as the novelist is concerned, quite beside the point. But it will surely mean much to the reader. He has been granted the privilege, which only the creative artist can give him, and the literary artist more directly than any other, of looking into another man's soul, of seeing the world as another sees it, of sharing someone else's response to life, and that in the most vivid manner possible. It may be that the reader is horrified, shocked, at the least disturbed, by what he sees in the novelist's mind; but since it is an image of life, what he sees there is just as much a fact, to be taken into account when the debit-and-credit balance of life is drawn up, as any incident reported in the daily newspaper. And before the reader turns away from a novel in repudiation, let him first ask himself whether the image of life the novel contains is not also an image of his own life. If, confronted with the characters in a novel, he cannot say, 'Yes, if I am honest I must admit they are aspects of me,' let him be very careful before he decides that he cannot say, 'There, but for the grace of God, go I.'

In my view, in the years to come the novel is going to become more rather than less important to us. For it is likely, whatever name we give to the kind of society in which we find ourselves, that we are all going to live more regimented lives than our fathers did. Ours is the age of statistics, of the average, of the mean; the concept of Statistical Man has succeeded that of Economic Man. We are numbers on identity cards, the consumers of a calculated minimum intake of calories producing so many thousand man-hours' worth of work a year. In the eyes of our administrators we become more and more featureless, more and more identical; more and more we approximate to the little men in Isotype illustrations. All our activities have become, as it were, material for graphs. Individual differences, as far as government is concerned, are being ironed out. It is probably inevitable, a necessary consequence of modern methods of production and of large-scale administration and social legislation.

If the known social requirements and duties of a citizen can be reduced to a number of symbols, obviously the task of government is made the easier. And it is not only administration that demands such a conception of the social man. We can see the kind of people we are expected to be in advertisements and in films; the range offered us is admittedly not large. But the pressure of the forces of publicity are such that more and more people are being made to approximate to fewer and fewer types, that is to say to fewer and fewer variations from the statistical norm. This is true, it may be observed, both for the Soviet Union and the United States; in both countries the good citizen is he who is best adjusted, i.e. who conforms most unquestioningly, to the requirements of the prevailing system, the state in Russia, the great producing and selling enterprises in America.

But man, more than ever it needs emphasizing now, is not merely social man or statistical man. He is an individual, a person, with a soul to be saved and a private life, a person, moreover, who, when all the social services have done all they can for him, remains essentially naked and alone. It is a truth often forgotten by politicians, statisticians, producers of consumer goods and those who advertise them, forgotten because it is a truth highly inconvenient to them and their ends. It is all the more necessary that they should be continually reminded of it; and so must the individual be.

It is exactly here that the function of the novel, of imaginative literature generally, is so vital. The State, the political party or philosophy, the advertising agent, subordinate man to an abstraction; they take part of man's make-up and call it the whole of man. But their pretensions are exposed, or should be, by the novel, for the novel is a result of the solitary man communing with himself. Obstinately, relentlessly, the novelist brings back all the problems of life, all the facts of existence, to the one test: how they affect the individual, man as man, not man as a unit in society, a producer or consumer, or cog in a machine. He brings back everything to the test of individual emotional experience.

The Russians have a proverb—perhaps they have it no longer, since its truth accords ill with Marxism—'The heart of man is a dark forest.' Out of the dark forest emerges all that is good and evil in man; it is the central fact of his existence. And it is the novelist's province. No wonder, then, that one of the novelist's main themes has always been the relationship between the individual solitary man, man naked, with the dark forest in his heart, and the society in which he exists, which is necessarily always in danger of becoming rigid and impersonal. The novel, you might say, is a sort of resistance movement against rigid and impersonal concepts of man and his duties; and inevitably the novelist, as Graham Greene has suggested, is the devil's advocate against all those forces which would dam the springs of human sympathy.

That is what the novel continually ministers to: the enlargement of human sympathy; and sympathy implies identification with and imaginative understanding of another, putting oneself in someone else's place, as we say.

The qualities that make for creative reading should now, I think, be clear. The reader has two duties; and if 'duties' sounds too austere a word, it should be remembered that they are duties the reader owes both to himself, if he is to get the most out of his reading, and to the cause of good writing. In the act of reading, of course, the two qualities exist side by side and are exercised simultaneously, but they can here be isolated as (*a*) humility and (*b*) discrimination or criticism.

5

'Immoral' Novels and 'Unpleasant' Characters

Let us take humility first. For humility, other words might be substituted, such as open-mindedness, willingness to sympathize and understand, perhaps even sportsmanship. To bring humility, or any of the qualities that the word covers, to a book is much the most difficult part of reading; criticism without humility, for instance, is sterile, as the history of criticism shows. When the notorious anonymous critic in the *Quarterly Review* reviewed Keats' *Endymion* with the words, 'Back to your pills and poultices, Mr Keats', or when Clement Scott, of the *Daily Telegraph*, wrote of Ibsen's *Ghosts*, 'Handled by an egotist and a bungler, it is only a deplorably dull play', neither critic was displaying any kind of humility and the criticism that resulted was so much beside the point, so obviously and flagrantly wrong, that in the eyes of posterity the writers merely made fools of themselves. Yet both, on occasion and within their limitations, were good critics. Why on these occasions did they err?

Because the Quarterly Reviewer, confronted with Keats, and Scott, confronted with Ibsen, were faced with work of a kind entirely different from anything they had met before. Their minds were simply not flexible enough to take in, to appreciate a new experience of the order that Keats and Ibsen offered them. They came to the work of these new writers, not without standards to judge them by, but with the wrong standards. A hundred similar instances of lack of humility in the presence of new works of art resulting in fatuous criticisms could be quoted. I mention them merely to show that reading with humility is the most difficult part of reading, and also the most essential. Arnold Bennett, as a young man, noted for his private use the following conclusions that came to him after walking down the King's Road, Chelsea, one afternoon:

Every scene, even the commonest, is wonderful, if only one can detach oneself, casting off all memory of use and custom, and behold it (as it were) for the first time; in its right, authentic colours; without making comparisons. The novelist should cherish and burnish this faculty of seeing crudely, simply, artlessly, ignorantly; of seeing like a baby or a lunatic, who lives each moment by itself and tarnishes the present by no remembrance of the past.

The reader should cultivate the same quality in his reading. I know it is a counsel of perfection, but it must be striven for. From one point of view, the novelist's job is simply to be a convincing liar. If he does not convince, he is a bad novelist. When we were children reading *Robinson Crusoe* or *Gulliver's Travels* we accepted Defoe's and Swift's lies, whoppers though they are, whole-heartedly. When we are adults we can no longer accept the lie as an end in itself; and yet, while we are reading a novel, that is precisely what we must do. Coleridge spoke of 'that willing suspension of disbelief which constitutes poetic faith'. The art of the novelist consists in making that willing suspension of disbelief possible, but with any novel it can only happen to the reader *if he will let it*, if he will, as it were, empty his mind of everything that impedes its reception of the novel. He must, in a word, be passive while reading the novel. And this, I repeat, is extraordinarily difficult. So many factors conspire against it. There are all one's articles of belief, religious, political, moral, philosophical. They may be most fervently held; and yet, while reading, one's grip on them must be loosened. Otherwise it would be impossible for a Protestant or an agnostic to read with pleasure a Roman Catholic novel, for a socialist to appreciate a tory satirist like Evelyn Waugh, and so on.

Perhaps the commonest complaints made by readers who do not belong to the passionate few is that novels are often 'unpleasant' or 'immoral'. It is not at all a new or specifically modern complaint; after all, Flaubert was prosecuted for alleged indecency in *Madame Bovary* and a bishop wanted to burn *Jude the Obscure*. What these complaints usually boil down to is that the novelist has run counter to the reader's most cherished beliefs about life; the reader is outraged because he identifies these beliefs with himself and so feels himself threatened when they are. Not unnaturally, he reacts violently, perhaps abusively: I suppose all novelists who attempt honestly to portray life as they themselves see it get their quota of abusive and sometimes scurrilous letters. But while it is right for the reader to hold fast to his beliefs he should at least have the decency to credit the novelist with as much honesty and integrity as he credits himself. The novelist, as well as the reader, has the right to his beliefs. And often, of course, the reader's violent reaction to the pictures of life he finds in a novel is indicative of the insecurity of his own belief; he is not so sure of it as he would like to be.

Again, the untrained reader often confuses a picture of immorality in a novel with an approval or even an advocacy of immorality on the novelist's part. The unfairness of this needs no stressing, but it is probably the most common type of confusion into which readers of fiction fall. The error is obvious enough after the event. Take *Madame Bovary* as an example. It is plain a more moral novel was never written; it is an exposure of the results, in human misery, of a woman's wishful-thinking, of false values, almost clinical in its detachment. But Flaubert is dead, a classic, and therefore safe. Living novelists continue to suffer from the confusion.

A publisher showed me a letter from a clergyman *à propos* of the writings of Ernest Hemingway, a collection of whose work, he said, was not the sort of book one would expect to find in a clergyman's bookshelves. Why ever not? Indeed, one is tempted to say, 'If not in a clergyman's library where should one find Hemingway?' The collection in question included Hemingway's novel *Fiesta*. It is, if you like, a picture of immorality. The characters, American and English expatriates living in France, do no work that is noticeable, drink too much and are promiscuous. The best of them are men whose lives have been shattered by the 1914–18 war. All are unhappy. It is a laconic, brilliant, disillusioned, bitter book. The heart of the novel lies in Lady Brett Ashley's voluntary renouncement of a young bullfighter she has fallen in love with and who has fallen in love with her, because she sees that his association with her would ruin him. The meaning of the novel is contained in the following passage of dialogue between Brett and the hero-narrator Jake:

'You know it makes one feel rather good deciding not to be a bitch.'
'Yes.'
'It's sort of what we have instead of God.'
'Some people have God,' I said. 'Quite a lot.'
'He never worked very well with me.'
'Should we have another Martini?'

The theme of *Fiesta* is in fact the theme which has inspired so many of the best novels that were written between the two wars: the hapless condition of men and women without God, the inhabitants of what, after T. S. Eliot's poem on the same theme, we may call the Waste Land, people for whom life has all but lost its meaning as they drift purposelessly through it little better than automata, behaviouristic puppets salivating like Pavlov's dogs in reaction to a few external stimuli. A more important theme for the novelist can scarcely be imagined. But it would be foolish to expect a novel illustrating the theme to be 'pleasant'.

Another example of what one is sometimes inclined to think is a typical reaction of a certain kind of reader to new novels. Once in the BBC 'Critics' programme I reviewed Gabriel Chevallier's *The Euffe Inheritance*. We were enthusiastic about it, my colleagues in the programme and myself, because, unlike most contemporary novels, it is, besides being a most convincing picture of middle-class provincial French society, a conspicuously sunny book; one felt after reading it that one had been in the presence of a civilized, sceptical, humane mind, which, though quite without illusions, found both life and human beings good. We said as much in the broadcast. Within three days came a letter from a lady demanding to know why, since one of the most important characters was described as being unfaithful to his wife, I could have called *The Euffe Inheritance* happy and sunny. I fancy M. Chevallier might have retorted that the English were notorious for their hypocrisy and that they ordered these things differently in France.

Allied to the unpleasant subject, the unpleasant picture of life, is the unpleasant character, who is another common bogy with untrained readers. 'Why do you write,' nearly every novelist must have been asked, 'about such unpleasant people?' The question is, of course, naïve, but it has been answered once and for all by two of our greatest woman novelists. This is what Charlotte Brontë said about her sister's *Wuthering Heights:*

Whether it is right or advisable to create beings like Heathcliff, I do not know: I scarcely think it is. But this I know: the writer who possesses the creative gifts owns something of which he is not always master—something that, at times, strangely wills and works for itself. . . . Be the work grim or glorious, dread or divine, you have little choice left but quiescent adoption. As for you—the nominal artist—your share in it has been to work passively under dictates you neither delivered nor could question—that would not be uttered at your prayer, nor suppressed nor changed at your caprice. If the result be attractive, the World will praise you; if it be repulsive, the same World will blame you, who almost as little deserve blame.

And here is the evidence of George Eliot, in *Adam Bede*:

'This Rector of Broxton is little better than a pagan!' I hear one of my readers exclaim. 'How much more edifying it would have been if you had made him give Arthur some truly spiritual advice. You might have put into his mouth the most beautiful things—quite as good as reading a sermon!'

Certainly I could, if I held it the highest vocation of the novelist to represent living things as they never have been and never will be. Then, of course, I might refashion life and character entirely after my own thinking; I might select the most unexceptional type of clergyman and put my own admirable opinions into his mouth on all occasions. But it happens, on the contrary, that my strongest effort is to avoid any such arbitrary picture, and to give a faithful account of men and things as they have mirrored themselves in my mind. The mind is doubtless defective; the outlines will sometimes be disturbed, the reflection faint or confused; but I feel as much bound to tell you as precisely as I can what that reflection is, as if I were in the witness-box narrating my experience on oath.

In short, then, a novelist's characters are not wholly in his control and he must not fake in order to produce pleasant characters for the sake of producing pleasant characters.

But there is another reason why, as has often been pointed out, the unpleasant characters in fiction are generally so much more convincing than the pleasant or the good. In the deeper sense, every good novel is autobiographical, and the characters, even though the novelist may believe he has taken them from life, are facets of his own character, manifestations of the sub-personalities that we all have and that we normally suppress. Now, just as no man is a hero to his valet so no man can be a hero to himself if he is at all sensitive and self-critical. M. Mauriac, in his profound essay *God and Mammon*, has noted the inability of novelists to portray saints; they draw, he says, 'creatures who are sublime and angelic but not human'. They fail because even the saints, as their lives show, 'believe themselves to be wretched; in fact, they *are* wretched, and it is precisely their sanctity that makes them see it so lucidly. They see what man, as compared with the light of God, really is even when sanctified, and they are horrified.' One need not be a Catholic, I think, or even a Christian, to agree with M. Mauriac's diagnosis.

The inference from all this surely is that the reader, if he asks that a novel should give, in George Eliot's words, a faithful account of man and things as they have mirrored themselves in his mind, cannot expect all the time to have pleasant books and pleasant characters. He must, if only as a measure of sportsmanship, admit the novelist's right and his duty to portray the world as he sees it, *no matter how repugnant that vision may be to the reader*. If it is repugnant, I suggest that the reader whose mind is not wholly closed should, in the interest of truth, scrutinize his own conclusions about life in the light of the novelist's vision. He may find it a necessary and powerful corrective to his own partial picture. Indeed, I am not certain that every novel that pretends to truth is not in some measure shocking. I do not mean that in any crude sense, but simply that any good novel will challenge the reader's preconceptions about life and human nature.

And there is one overriding fact that all readers of contemporary fiction should remember. Mr Eliot has stated it in these words: 'Every age gets the art it deserves, and every age must accept the art it gets.'

6

The Challenge from the Past

So FAR I have discussed readers' reactions to contemporary fiction only. Their reactions to the fiction of the past do not differ greatly. How often has one heard academic critics deplore those qualities in the work of classic writers which they find unpleasant. Even Shakespeare is not exempt. He is found to be dirty, and very pessimistic. Fielding is coarse, Sterne smutty. The great Victorians are often prigs and sometimes snobs and too inclined to be squeamish in matters of sex. Such statements of opinion, unless expressed with great circumspection, are obviously as provincial—for there is such a thing as being provincial in time as well as in place—as the reactions to the 'unpleasantness' of contemporary novels. They spring from the same source, an inability on the reader's part to submit himself whole-heartedly to the work being read.

It is scarcely for the twentieth, of all centuries, to set itself up to judge the morals, manners and customs of previous ages; but to do so, and to condemn work of the past which offends our own taste, is to fail to appreciate the very feel of the past, which is incarnate in its fiction as in nowhere else. It is to be deficient in sympathy, and where there is deficiency in sympathy criticism too will be deficient. Of course Shakespeare is sometimes dirty, Fielding coarse, Sterne smutty, the Victorians often prigs, snobs and squeamish. All these attributes are part and parcel of the intellectual and emotional climate of their periods; without them, they would be not more but less than they are.

Much of the difficulty readers find in contemporary fiction arises from their unwillingness to accept the age in which they live. The difficulty some readers find in reading the fiction of the past arises from an inability to see the past as it was; it is much simpler to read into it our own preconceived opinions about it, often enough derived from quite inferior sources such as historical films or muddled memories of what we learnt at school. Think how, a few years ago, the single word 'Victorian' was used to damn the whole of the nineteenth century. It is quite useless to hope to read the great nineteenth century novelists if you approach them with your mind already made up that the Victorians were funny old men with beards, who hid the legs of pianos with draperies.

The first essential in reading the novelists of the past is to realize that they were men quite as intelligent and sensitive as the reader and that they were writing for a public at least as shrewd and sensible as a modern public. Their preoccupations were not those of the modern novelist, and just for that reason, because we can read them in a much more detached way than we read contemporary work, they can throw new light for us on human nature and on society; or rather, they bring back to us facets of human nature and society that we, with our contemporary preoccupations, tend to forget. It is for this reason that the sensitive reader will find the classic novelist quite as shocking in the best sense, as disturbing, as the best contemporary writers. He will disturb our complacency no less than they. The view of human passion expressed in *Wuthering Heights*, for instance, is as challenging as that presented in the novels of D. H. Lawrence. To read Dickens is to plunge into a nightmare world quite as violent and terrifying as Graham Greene's; and Jane Austen exposes the economic basis of society with a coolness and acceptance that make the work of Marxist novelists appear hysterical by comparison. Similarly, as long as there is a class system, of whatever sort it may be, and there are men and women who feel themselves uprooted from their origins and socially maladjusted, novels like Gissing's *The Odd Women* and *Born in Exile* will continue to astonish and disturb because of the very force and intransigence with which their author exposes the wretchedness of the unclassed.

Of course the conventions that the novelists of the past follow, the language they use, differ from those of modern novelists; but they can be easily learned. All that is wanted is the quality without which all reading is fruitless, humility.

7

A Basis for Judgment

WE CAN now discuss the problem of reading with discrimination, reading critically. I have, of course, made a convenient distinction between reading with humility and reading critically which should not exist in fact. The reader who reads with humility alone may be nothing more than an undiscriminating consumer of the literary fare put before him. Reading a book is an experience, but some experiences are more valuable than others, and when the reading is completed the value of what has been read must be determined. Plainly, to make a fully balanced estimate on a novel a wide knowledge of other novels, past and present, is needed.

To take a very simple instance: a reader who has read only *The Good Companions* can scarcely estimate its worth as accurately as a reader who has also read *Nicholas Nickleby*. Behind all contemporary work stand the giants of the past, from Defoe to Flaubert, Tolstoy, Hardy and Henry James, with whom it has to be brought into some kind of relation. One cannot have one standard of judgment for the work of the past and another for the work of the present. The basis of all criticism is comparison,

comparison with the best achievements in the particular medium being criticized. And this is one reason why the reader should mingle his reading of modern fiction as much as possible with a reading of the classic novels, for ultimately they are the tests by which contemporary work must be judged.

Criticism, in other words, is a branch of scholarship, and criticism of this kind is obviously beyond the reach of the ordinary reader. But there is another test, beside that of scholarship, which it is in the power of every reader to bring to the fiction he reads. The classic novels are classics because of the illumination of life they offer. They are statements about human nature, made in terms of story and character, which have stood the test of time, have withstood the scrutiny of successive generations of readers. But once they were new books and what the passionate few who read them then had to decide was how far they were true to human nature, how far they were true to experience. This is precisely what the modern reader has to do when he reads a modern novel. Intelligent reading of a modern novel will prompt the following questions in a reader's mind: Does this novelist's view of life, as expressed in this book, square with the essential facts of life as I myself have known them? Does it fall short of them? Does it seem false to them? Does it lead me to question my own experience of life? Shall I have to revise or amplify my view of life as a result of reading this novel?

There is nothing esoteric about such questions. We are all of us every day constantly summing up people and situations in the light of our previous experience of life. All the facts about human nature are to hand; we have only to look about us at our neighbours, our friends, our enemies; we have only to look into ourselves. Interpretation of the facts is a different matter, of course, for there are as many differences of interpretation as there are human beings in the world. Even so, our interpretation of the facts is a result of our experience of life, though I need hardly say that experience is not merely what happens to us but is the intangible quality born of the marriage between what happens to us and the way in which we react towards it. It is that experience—and the books we read go to make that

experience as much as being in love or being bombed in a blitz—which we must bring to our reading. What the novelist asks of his reader is that he should be as sincere with himself in evaluating the book as the novelist was in writing it.

This task of evaluation is obviously in the reader's own interest; in no other way can he discriminate, and without discrimination there can be no gradations of pleasure. Does it sound highbrow? It is not at all: or if it is, then highbrows are more common than is sometimes imagined, which is what indeed I believe. The reader is merely invited to bring to the novels he reads the same care for excellence, the same sense of the virtue of comparison, that he takes to a football match on Saturday afternoon. Watch a crowd of football fans; listen to them in the pub discussing the game afterwards: there are highbrows for you. They display the same concern for standards, the same passionate refusal to put up with the third-rate when the best is available, which distinguishes the few who care passionately about books. All that is different are the terms of reference; in discussion of football the reference is to the elements in a complex pattern of movement; in discussion of books the final reference is to life, to the experience which all men share and none can escape.

But the exercise of the critical faculty not only increases the reader's pleasure; it is also a duty that the reader owes to good writing. A footballer who is unsportsmanlike or disregards the rules of the game, is booed. The novelist, too, has his obligations to art, which is as much as to say his obligations to the tradition of the novel and to the novel of the future. The first of these is to be honest to his experience of life, to remember, as George Eliot said, that he is as much bound to tell you as precisely as he can what the reflection of men and things that has mirrored itself in his mind is, as if he were in the witness-box narrating his experience on oath. We call this the novelist's integrity; and it is up to the reader to see that novelists keep their integrity, by shunning those who do not. If the novelist tries to fake the findings of his experience, no matter for what reason, whether for money or in the hope of pleasing a large public, whether to make converts to his religion or propaganda for his political party, he is being dishonest as a novelist and has lost his integrity, and he should be shunned.

The reader's duty is no less than the novelist's here, for by his encouragement, his sympathy with honest endeavour, his insistence that the novelist should regard him as an adult who is also interested in truth for its own sake, he can bring about the mental atmosphere that makes the writing of honest novels not an isolated activity carried on against the grain of the times, as it largely is today, but in the truest sense a willing collaboration between writer and reader.

8

Seven Novels Discussed

I. The Power and the Glory
Graham Greene

So far I have discussed reading in general terms. Now I want to take seven works of fiction, as specimens, as it were, and try to bring out what the reader who is willing to read with humility may find in them and how he should approach them.

Let us begin with an adventure-story, *The Power and the Glory*, by Graham Greene, the story of a chase, of a fugitive evading the police; almost the oldest kind of adventure story; and set in Mexico, surely a romantic enough background. But consider the title, which is often the novelist's own summary of the theme he is treating and the way he regards that theme, though it should be remembered that not all good novels have good titles. Well, confronted with the title *The Power and the Glory*, the reader cannot fail to supply the context of the phrase, 'For Thine is the kingdom . . .'; and with the Lord's Prayer in his mind he will scarcely expect a conventional adventure story. And this impression will be reinforced by the quotation from Dryden Mr Greene has put on the title-page:

> Th' inclosure narrowed; the sagacious power
> Of hounds and death drew nearer every hour.

The reader has not yet begun to read; but from the title and the epigraph he will already have caught something of the mood of the novel. To that extent he will be in tune with the author. He will obviously be jarred if, when he begins to read, he finds the novel frivolous or trivial. For the very fact of the title chosen and the epigraph added is a sort of guarantee to the reader that the novelist is essaying a subject of high seriousness.

But let us turn to the first page, the first paragraph:

> Mr Tench went out to look for his ether cylinder: out into the blazing Mexican sun and the bleaching dust. A few buzzards looked down from the roof with shabby indifference: he wasn't carrion yet. A faint feeling of rebellion stirred in Mr Tench's heart, and he wrenched up a piece of the road with splintering finger-nails and tossed it feebly up at them. One of them rose and flapped across the town: over the tiny plaza, over the bust of an ex-president, ex-general, ex-human being, over the two stalls which sold mineral water, towards the river and the sea. It wouldn't find anything there: the sharks looked after the carrion on that side. Mr Tench went on across the plaza.
>
> He said 'Buenos dias' to a man with a gun who sat in a small patch of shade against a wall. But it wasn't like England: the man said nothing at all, just stared malevolently up at Mr Tench, as if he had never had any dealings with the foreigner, as if Mr Tench were not responsible for his two gold bicuspid teeth. . . .

From these first two hundred words of the novel the reader will already have gained a lot. Obviously Mr Greene's Mexico has nothing in common with the conventional idea of Mexico, the Mexico of technicolor musicals and the dance bands of the Light Programme; it is savagely hot, depressed, squalid. But the reader will have noticed something else. Mr Greene is conveying Mexico to us not through straight, objective description. We are being shown the country, the small town, through a powerful temperament: buzzards, carrion, shabby indifference, splintering finger-nails, an ex-human being, sharks, malevolence: these are the keywords by which Mr Greene rapidly evokes an image of disgust, of hopelessness. It may be, of course, that the image is merely of Mr Tench's disgust and hopelessness, not of the author's own reaction to Mexico. To decide that the reader must read further.

When he does, he will find that, just as the setting is not in the least romantic, so the hero, the fugitive, is not in the least the conventional hero of the adventure story of pursuit. He is, in the first place, a priest, for the action takes place in a Mexican State in which, at the time of the events described, the church was banned, its priests outlawed. The priest, then, is a representative of an underground resistance movement; and the reader will almost inevitably think of later underground movements in other totalitarian countries, and remembering stories of the Maquis, for instance, he may expect a relation of heroism. But the priest is far from being an heroic figure; he is a bad priest, a whisky priest; he has lived with a woman who has had a child by him; he can keep going only on alcohol. If you combed the world you could scarcely find a worse priest. It is plain that *The Power and the Glory* is an anti-romantic novel, that Mr Greene is out to destroy any illusions we may possess either about Mexico or the automatic goodness of priests. Yet his priest, because of the situation he finds himself in, and because he is a priest called upon to fulfil the duties of his priestly office, does become a hero, though in the least heroic way. Indeed, he becomes more than a hero. We realize, at the end of the book, that he is a martyr, perhaps a saint, and none the less so because martyrdom and sainthood have been thrust upon him.

Reading this sketchy account of *The Power and the Glory*, the reader may ask: 'Why should this story of a remote corner of Mexico, which is itself remote enough, mean anything to me?' The answer is that the story transcends its setting, its local habitation. Mr Greene brings us Mexico in all its heat and stink and poverty, but the novel is only incidentally concerned with that country. This is even more obvious now than it was when the novel was published, in 1940. For, opposed to the priest is another character, the police lieutenant. He, too, is a dedicated spirit, but not to God; rather to something we might call the social conscience. From almost every secular point of view he is a much more worthy person than the priest: he is the practical idealist, the planner with a vision of the good society. The whole conflict between the two men and the views of life and death they stand for, indeed, the very heart of the book, is exposed when they are face to face with each other, the priest a prisoner awaiting death, the lieutenant his gaoler:

'Well, we have ideas, too,' the lieutenant was saying. 'No more money for saying prayers, no more money for building places to say prayers in. We'll give people food instead, teach them to read, give them books. We'll see they don't suffer.'

'But if they want to suffer. . . .'

'A man may want to rape a woman. Are we to allow it because he wants to? Suffering is wrong.'

'And you suffer all the time,' the priest commented, watching the sour Indian face behind the candle-flame. He said: 'It sounds fine, doesn't it? Does the jefe feel like that, too?'

'Oh, we have our bad men.'

'And what happens afterwards? I mean after everybody has got enough to eat and can read the right books—the books you let them read?'

'Nothing. Death's a fact. We don't try to alter facts.'

'We agree about a lot of things,' the priest said, idly dealing out his card. 'We have facts, too, we don't try to alter—that the world's unhappy whether you are rich or poor—unless you are a saint, and there aren't many of those. It's not worth bothering too much about a little pain here. There's one belief we both of us have—that we'll all be dead in a hundred years.' He fumbled, trying to shuffle, and bent his cards: his hands were not steady.

'All the same, you're worried now about a little pain,' the lieutenant said maliciously, watching his fingers.

'But I'm not a saint,' the priest said. 'I'm not even a brave man.' He looked up apprehensively: light was coming back: the candle was no longer necessary. It would soon be clear enough to start the long journey back. He felt a desire to go on talking, to delay even by a few minutes the decision to start. He said: 'That's another difference between us. It's no good your working for your end unless you're a good man yourself. And there won't always be good men in your party. Then you'll have all the old starvation, beating, get-rich-anyhow. But it doesn't matter so much my being a coward—

and all the rest. I can put God into a man's mouth just the same—and I can give him God's pardon. It wouldn't make any difference to that if every priest in the Church was like me.'

That surely goes to the core of the main conflict of our time. There, succinctly stated, is the real issue between the Marxists and the Christian tradition. There is more to it than that, of course; as the title itself would indicate, even if it weren't explicit in the book, the priest's fundamental heroism is given to him by God; ultimately, he has a source of power denied to the police lieutenant. But the conflict, which is now world-wide, is the more powerfully stated in Mr Greene's novel just because it is stated in terms of fiction; its vision is more complete just because the priest is consciously unheroic, knows himself a coward.

How does Mr Greene achieve the terrific power of the illusion he imposes upon us? That is a matter of style and technique. There are few factors in writing more generally misunderstood than style. It is sometimes thought of as something added to expression, an ornamental quality, a French polish given to the writer's words for the sake of decoration. Nothing could be more false. In fact, expression itself is style. Someone once said: 'Style is the man [i.e. the writer] himself.' It is the most hackneyed of quotations, but it still expresses the final truth about style. Style is always highly personal, because it is organic to the writer; he can no more change it than he can change the bone-structure of his face.

I do not, of course, intend to imply that a novelist is the passive victim of his style. It is something to be exercised; its scope and suppleness can be increased with practice; but the limits and range of a man's style are fixed by his character and temperament. There is an obvious analogy with the style of cricketers. One thing is certain: the more intense a novelist's vision, the more urgent his desire to communicate what he has seen, so the more effective he will seek to make his style. Mr Greene's is as individual as one would expect from so individual a temperament. I do not think Mr Greene's vision has changed substantially in the twenty-five and more years in which he has been writing; he has always seen this world as a seedily meaningless wasteland and its inhabitants as futile and evil unless existing in relation to something outside them and transcending them, such as an ideal like loyalty or stoical endurance and, in his later books, God. But he has sought continually to make his style a more precise instrument by which to render his vision and fix it indelibly in the reader's mind. He has learned much from the films; his style, economical, laconic, swift-moving, is a succession of images of ugliness, squalor and disgust which are as vivid and as surely placed in their context to rivet the reader's attention as the images in a film. He does not need to comment on the world he puts before us in fiction; the style itself is the comment.

II. Between the Acts
Virginia Woolf

Let us now turn to another novel, *Between the Acts*, the last book Mrs Virginia Woolf wrote before she died. By the time you have read twenty pages the setting and events which will take place have established themselves. The scene is a country-house, inhabited by old Mr Oliver and his sister Mrs Swithin, Mr Oliver's son and Isa his wife and their children. Isa is perhaps in love with, certainly attracted by, a neighbouring farmer. There is to be a pageant in the grounds. And already, having related the plot thus far, I hear the reader protest: 'The quiet lives of comfortable people. Small talk in a country-house. Pretty small beer, isn't it? And surely I've read that novel before.' Well, on the third page occurs the following passage. Old Mr Oliver has just quoted two lines from a lyric of Byron's:

> Isa raised her head. The words made two rings, perfect rings, that floated them, herself and Haines, like two swans down stream. But his snow-white breast was circled with a tangle of dirty duckweed; and she, too, in her webbed feet was entangled, by her husband, the stockbroker.

Is not that vivid and beautiful image a clue to Mrs Woolf's intentions? She is using prose; but all the same she is writing poetically. By the third page, then, the reader need have no doubts: he is not going to read a conventional country-house novel of small talk among the comfortable. Then four pages later we meet old Mrs Swithin; it is the morning after. I shall quote the whole passage, because it is so excellent an example of Mrs Woolf's method:

But it was summer now. She had been waked by the birds. How they sang! attacking the dawn like so many choir-boys attacking an iced cake. Forced to listen, she had stretched for her favourite reading—an Outline of History—and had spent the hours between three and five thinking of rhododendron forests in Piccadilly; when the entire continent, not then, she understood, divided by a channel, was all one; populated, she understood, by elephant-bodied, seal-necked, heaving, surging, slowly writhing, and, she supposed, barking monsters; the iguanodon, the mammoth, and the mastodon; from whom presumably, she thought, jerking the window open, we descend.

It took her five seconds in actual time, in mind time ever so much longer, to separate Grace herself, with blue china on a tray, from the leather-covered grunting monster who was about, as the door opened, to demolish a whole tree in the green steaming undergrowth of the primeval forest. Naturally, she jumped, as Grace put the tray down and said: 'Good morning, Ma'am.' 'Batty,' Grace called her, as she felt on her face the divided glance that was half meant for a beast in a swamp, half for a maid in a print frock and white apron.

'How these birds sing!' said Mrs Swithin, at a venture. The window was open now; the birds certainly were singing. An obliging thrush hopped across the lawn; a coil of pinkish rubber twisted in its beak. Tempted by the sight to continue her imaginative reconstruction of the past, Mrs Swithin paused; she was given to increasing the bounds of the moment by flights into past or future; but she remembered her mother—her mother in that very room rebuking her. 'Don't stand gaping, Lucy, or the wind'll change. . . .' How often her mother had rebuked her in that room—'but in a very different world,' as her brother would remind her. So she sat down to morning tea, like any other old lady with a high nose, thin cheeks, a ring on her finger and the usual trappings of rather shabby but gallant old age, which included in her case a cross gleaming gold on her breast.

To the experienced reader such a passage, coming so early in the novel, will be full of information, not merely about the character of Mrs Swithin but about Mrs Woolf's intentions in the novel. For in a good novel nothing is there by accident. In the passage quoted we are presented with Mrs Swithin. We find her favourite reading is in popular outlines of pre-history; her imagination is such that when the maid suddenly appears she does not for a moment know where she is, in the past or the present. Now this preoccupation with pre-history may be merely an indication of Mrs Swithin's character or it may be a device of Mrs Woolf's whereby she may economically, and without shifting her theme from the tiny stage of the country-house, set her action against the whole background of the history of life. Before we can decide that we must read further, but the possibility is one that the experienced reader would keep in mind. I think, even on the evidence of that passage alone, he would incline to think that the latter was indeed Mrs Woolf's purpose, for he would note that in it Mrs Woolf showed her delight in ranging backwards and forwards in time; for besides the rhododendron forest in Piccadilly we are given a glimpse of Mrs Swithin as a child, as a child 'in a very different world'. He would realize that Mrs Woolf was concerned with the flux, the ceaseless change, of life, that it was her practice to set what she calls 'actual time' against 'mind time'.

Those would not be the only impressions he would take away from the passage. He would observe that Mrs Woolf's touch is light, that she glances at, rather than stresses, the subjects which pre-occupy her mind, that what she writes is bathed in the light of a whimsical darting humour. He would be quite certain that, in *Between the Acts* at any rate, it was not Mrs Woolf's intention to build a solid world, and if momentarily he felt like comparing her with Sinclair Lewis, who does precisely that in his best novels, he would remember that, as Longfellow portentously said, 'things are not what they seem' and that to the physicist, for instance, the solid world is anything but solid but exists, like Mrs Woolf's, in a condition of unceasing flux.

And with the character of Mrs Swithin in mind, he would,

I think, expect a not wholly conventional pageant from Mrs Woolf. The pageant, acted by the villagers, is a delightfully brilliant parody of a village pageant. Mrs Woolf uses the stock notions of English history; but, as the reader will soon discover, it has a meaning beyond the surface meaning. Just as the ultimate background of the book is Mrs Swithin's vision of the whole development of life on the earth, so the nearer background is the development of England. It is kept deliberately light; otherwise it would be too heavy a burden for the fragile structure of Mrs Woolf's plot. Isa and her husband must be reconciled; and so we come to the last page. It is night.

Lucy (Mrs Swithin) turned the page, quickly, guiltily, like a child who will be told to go to bed before the end of the chapter.

'Prehistoric man,' she read, 'half-human, half-ape, roused himself from his semi-crouching position and raised great stones.'

She slipped the letter from Scarborough between the pages to mark the end of the chapter, rose, smiled, and tiptoed silently out of the room.

The old people had gone up to bed. Giles crumpled the newspaper and turned out the light. Left alone together for the first time that day, they were silent. Alone, enmity was bared; also love. Before they slept, they must fight; after they had fought, they would embrace. From that embrace another life might be born. But first they must fight, as the dog fox fights with the vixen, in the heart of darkness, in the fields of night.

Isa let her sewing drop. The great hooded chairs had become enormous. And Giles, too. And Isa, too, against the window. The window was all sky without colour. The house had lost its shelter. It was night before roads were made, or houses. It was the night that dwellers in caves had watched from some high place among rocks.

Then the curtain rose. They spoke.

In our minds, psychologists say, is stored in the shape of myth and dream the whole history of the race. What Mrs Woolf has done is to recapitulate, as it were in capsule form, in the setting of a summer day in an English country house just before the war, the whole epic of the human story, racial no less than national. In terms of modern people in a modern setting, she has shown us the continuity of life, man as the inheritor of all the past.

She does something else, too. There is the character of Miss La Trobe, the pageant-mistress. Miss La Trobe is no less than the eternal artist, with a vision to express. She might be the Stevenson I quoted from at the beginning of this little book, or Mrs Woolf herself. For the other characters the pageant is just an entertainment; for Miss La Trobe it is an act of creation:

> Hadn't she, for twenty-five minutes, made them see? A vision imparted was relief from agony . . . for one moment . . . for one moment. . . . She heard the breeze rustle in the branches. She saw Giles Oliver with his back to the audience. Also Cobbet of Cobbs Corner. She hadn't made them see. It was a failure, another damned failure! As usual. Her vision escaped her. And turning, she strode to the actors, undressing, down in the hollow, where butterflies feast upon swords of silver paper; where the dishcloths in the shadow made pools of yellow.

Through the character of Miss La Trobe and her pageant, exercise in doggerel as it mainly is, Mrs Woolf states the truth about the artist and his unceasing endeavour to make his audience see which T. S. Eliot expresses in *East Coker* in the words, 'Every attempt is a wholly new start, and a different kind of failure.'

III. MIDDLEMARCH
GEORGE ELIOT

The Power and the Glory and *Between the Acts* may or may not become classics, though they are certainly among the finest novels of our time. Let us now look at a novel whose classic stature is not in doubt, a book which many readers consider the greatest English novel: George Eliot's *Middlemarch*. One striking difference between this novel and those of our contemporaries the reader will immediately recognize, quite apart from the sheer physical difference in size. This is the difference between George Eliot's attitude to her characters and that of most contemporary writers. The contemporary novelist strives as much as he can to break down the barriers between the reader and his characters.

It is in a sense the difference between personages seen on the film and personages seen on the stage. The cinematograph operator projects the film so that the characters are before the spectator's very eyes; but the characters in a stage play are always at a further remove from us: there are the footlights between us and them; we see them as though they were in a world apart from us; we are, so to speak, privileged Peeping Toms watching the behaviour of people who are unaware that one wall of the house they inhabit has been knocked down. The analogy is not perfect, but the contemporary novelist aims at showing us the very thoughts and feelings of his characters with the immediacy of the film; he plunges us into the stream of their thoughts and sensations: remember Greene's Mr Tench, Mrs Woolf's Mrs Swithin.

This is not George Eliot's way, nor that of any other English novelist of her time or before her. George Eliot tells us much more, in her own voice, about her characters than any modern novelist would. It is she who tells us what they think and feel, and she comments on their thinking and feeling; she passes judgment on them continually, interrupts the action to deduce a general law from what one of them has said or done. She is omniscient where they are concerned; she is much nearer to the oral teller of stories than is the contemporary novelist. When he comments on his action he rarely does it in his own person, but rather by a skilful choice and juxtaposition of images; so, in the first chapter of *The Power and the Glory*, Greene does not say in as many words that the scene is sordid; the reader is allowed to gather that from Greene's description, precisely as he would from the opening shots of a film.

I am not concerned to defend or justify one attitude towards the novelist's characters as against the other. Many modern readers object to George Eliot's moralizing on her characters; in the case of some of her contemporaries, Thackeray in particular, such objections are well merited. But the gain is not necessarily the modern novelist's, because, though his method makes for immediacy, George Eliot's has the advantage of putting the characters at a distance from the reader. This can be expressed in another way. The reader of a modern novel is in much the same position as the spectator in a cinema: he is watching an action which is going on as he watches. In a novel like *Middlemarch*, the action has been completed before the reader takes the book up; George Eliot is telling him of what has already happened and therefore, as she describes the characters and their doings, she interprets them, moralizes about them, generalizes on them while she is reporting her story. This is a very real difference, which must be remembered when the reader turns from modern fiction to the work of the past.

It makes her novel much more leisurely. It also results, I think, in our knowing her characters more thoroughly than we do those of most modern novelists, though we may not know them as intimately; for we have very much more time in which to get to know them. This is a test both of the novelist and of the reader; the relatively slow pace of most nineteenth-century novels means that the writer may become a bore and the reader bored. I think the danger is less in the case of George Eliot than with some of her contemporaries because of the quality of her mind. It is ponderous, as her style is ponderous, but it is also noble. She is the novelist of conscience, and that constitutes one of the most attractive qualities of her work today. Dorothea Brooke, the heroine of *Middlemarch*, is both beautiful and serious, of a piece with the book's opening sentences:

> Miss Brooke had that kind of beauty which seems to be thrown into relief by poor dress. Her hand and wrist were so finely formed that she could wear sleeves not less bare of style than those in which the Blessed Virgin appeared to Italian painters; and her profile as well as her stature and bearing seemed to gain the more dignity from her plain garments, which by the side of provincial fashion gave her the impressiveness of a fine quotation from the Bible—or from one of our elder poets—in a paragraph of today's newspaper.

This passage describes not only Dorothea's quality but also much of George Eliot's as a novelist. One says much and not all because though she was a moralist who believed inflexibly that what befell a man was the result of his own actions, of his own character, she was also a humorist, as is strikingly obvious as early on in the novel as the beginning of the second chapter.

She is indeed a great humorous novelist; her vignettes of simple, shrewd country folk are unsurpassed; but the humour is always in the service of, subdued by, her high seriousness. She laughs gently at Dorothea Brooke's lofty ideals, but she also takes them deadly seriously.

So the reader's main task when he takes up *Middlemarch* is to get himself acclimatized to a tempo and a seriousness of a kind different from those he is accustomed to. One cannot say that George Eliot is more serious than the best novelists of our own day; that would be absurd; but her seriousness is unlike theirs. It is a seriousness arising out of moral certainty, which is plainly the quality in which our own age is most conspicuously lacking. It is a quality of which we are perhaps somewhat suspicious.

The reader must be prepared to find George Eliot judging her characters, weighing them in the balance and approving them or finding them wanting, in a way in which no modern novelist would ever do, except by implication. But it is this very certainty of her moral judgments, her certainty that she knows what is right and what is wrong, which helps George Eliot to create her wonderfully solid world, the completest picture of life in provincial England at any one given time that any English novelist has given us. But, for a time at any rate, a patient submission on the part of the reader may be necessary; one must read on until—one realizes it suddenly, though it is the fruit of application—one finds one has, as it were, lived oneself into George Eliot's world. It is, in *Middlemarch* especially, a most richly rewarding world inhabited by characters as real as any in fiction. And the reader will find George Eliot's assumptions, even though it may be impossible for him to share them, the most damaging criticism possible of the world he himself lives in. Every generation in turn has to test the classics for itself; but every generation in turns finds in the classics its own most searching test; and the great value of George Eliot to us at this time is that her novels, and *Middlemarch* in particular, with their severe but humane moral basis, correct our own obsessions and expose our inadequacies both as men and novelists.

IV. The Masters
C. P. Snow

Novels, I have said, are mainly about people; they are inhabited by recognizable men and women. Men and women exist in relation to one another, but they also exist in relation to the community of which they are part. Novels dealing with relations between people in their private aspects, novels of personal relationships, are numerous in contemporary English fiction. Novels dealing with people in relation to the community are much less common and therefore, when they occur, the more precious. Here, it must be admitted, we compare badly with contemporary American fiction. It has been said that the great traditional theme of the American novel is, simply, what it means to be, what is involved in being, an American; and if this is so, as it seems to me it largely is, then plainly characters in much of the best American fiction exist in a dimension beyond the purely personal.

An English novel whose theme is men living in a community is C. P. Snow's *The Masters*. This is one of a series of novels C. P. Snow is writing which together will compose the history of a representative man of our time, the narrator Lewis Eliot; a representative man but a remarkable one in that his career has impinged upon the life of his time at many points, for, by profession a barrister, he has been a law lecturer at Cambridge and, in the later works, is a senior civil servant. I find the novels that make up the series so far as it has gone uneven in quality, but *The Masters* is certainly one of the most impressive that has been published in England since the war, and one reason for its weight and authority is that the characters exist in a dimension beyond the personal.

Of course, *The Masters* is, among other things, a study in human relationships. The scene is a college at Cambridge just before the war, but the characters are restricted almost entirely to the fellows of the college; I don't think that a single undergraduate, for instance, appears as a character. It is a study, then, of men living together in what to the outside world must appear very much a closed community; they are bound to each other not necessarily by affection or friendship but by loyalty to an institution and the observance of a common way of life, a way of life traditional and ritualistic, rooted in history.

Simply as a recreation of life in an English college, life as lived by the inhabitants of the Senior Common Room, I know of no novel in English with which *The Masters* may be compared. This itself is much, for one of the ends of fiction must be, as Dr Johnson said of poetry, to make new things familiar. But this in a sense is only the beginning of C. P. Snow's intentions. When the novel opens we learn that the Master has an incurable disease and that his death must be a matter of months, and the knowledge of this immediately changes the long-established relations of the dons one to another. A new Master must be elected, chosen if possible from among the dons themselves. Who is it to be? Cliques, caucuses and factions reveal themselves almost overnight; rival candidates are put forward with equal sincerity and conviction by their partisans; the harmony of the college is shattered into fragments, old friendships are broken, and old jealousies, antipathies, grudges re-assert themselves. We realize that what we are reading is not only a study of human relations but also a study of a man as a political animal; we are confronted with the necessary preliminaries to the practice of government.

Politics implies the exercise of power, veiled or otherwise, and one of the most striking sources of C. P. Snow's strength as a novelist is his knowledge of the various ways in which men are moved by the quest for power. And power takes many forms, as Snow shows us in his analysis of the characters of Dr Jago, one of the candidates for the Mastership, and of his partisans, Brown and Chrystal. Lewis Eliot, who is also of their party, sees them thus:

> I watched their heads, grouped round the table, their faces glowing with their purpose—Brown's purple-pink, rubicund, keen-eyed, Chrystal's beaky, domineering, Jago's pale, worn with the excesses of emotion, his eyes intensely lit. Each of these three was seeking power, I thought—but the power each wanted was as different as they were themselves. Brown's was one which no one need know but himself; he wanted to handle, coax, guide, contrive, so that men

found themselves in the places he had designed; he did not want an office or title to underline his power, it was good enough to sit back amiably and see it work.

Chrystal wanted to be no more than Dean, but he wanted the Dean, in this little empire of the college, to be known as a man of power. Less subtle, less reflective, more immediate than his friend, he needed the moment-by-moment sensation of power. He needed to feel that he was listened to, that he was commanding here and now, that his word was obeyed. Brown would be content to get Jago elected and influence him afterwards, no one but himself knowing how much he had done. That was too impalpable a satisfaction for Chrystal, Chrystal was impelled to have his own part recognized, by Jago, by Brown and the college. As we spoke that evening, it was essential for Chrystal that he should see this effect on Jago himself. He wanted nothing more than that, he was no more ambitious than Brown—but irresistibly he needed to see and feel his power.

Jago enjoyed the dramatic impact of power, like Chrystal: but he was seeking for other things besides. He was an ambitious man, as neither Brown nor Chrystal were. In any society, he would have longed to be first; and he would have longed for it because of everything that marked him out as different from the rest. He longed for all the trappings, titles, ornaments and show of power. He would love to hear himself called Master; he would love to begin a formal act at a college meeting 'I, Paul Jago, Master of the college. . . .' He wanted the grandeur of the Lodge, he wanted to be styled among the heads of houses. He enjoyed the prospect of an entry in the College history—'Dr P. Jago, 41st Master.' For him, in every word that separated the Master from his fellows, in every ornament of the Lodge, in every act of formal duty, there was a gleam of magic.

There was something else. He had just said to Chrystal 'we can make it a great college'. Like most ambitious men, he believed that there were things that only he could do. . . .

By the time we have finished reading *The Masters* we realize that we have seen the world under one of its aspects—the political—in microcosm. We have been shown what moves men when they act politically, that is in terms of the use of power that decides who shall rule. The restricted scene of the Cambridge common room mirrors the world, and we feel that the intrigues that go to the making of a party leader or a prime minister are no greater and no less than those shown here.

It is this that makes *The Masters* so satisfying a novel. One aspect of life has been illuminated. It is an aspect that has not often been shown in English fiction. The political novels of Trollope are played out on the outskirts of politics, and those of Wells are vitiated by his impatience with the manoeuvres attendant on politics. In the large sense, Disraeli is the English political novelist; but politics is not confined to Parliament and party: wherever there are men and institutions, men living in communities, there is politics. C. P. Snow uses a small community to illustrate the nature of politics generally. Yet there is this to be said. As a novel on the nature of politics *The Masters* would have failed had not its author firmly grasped as men the characters he describes. *The Masters* is a successful novel about politics because it is, in the first instance, a successful novel about life in a Cambridge college.

v. The Horse's Mouth
Joyce Cary

I suspect that fundamentally all writers belong to one or the other of two broadly opposed groups which were indicated by Coleridge when he compared and contrasted Shakespeare and Milton. 'While the former,' he said, 'darts himself forth, and passes into all the forms of human character and passion; the other attracts all forms and things to himself, into the unity of his own ideal. All things and modes of action shape themselves anew in the being of Milton; while Shakespeare becomes all things, yet for ever remaining himself.' We may take Shakespeare and Milton, then, as the two ideal types of these two great divisions into which writers fall. They are the literary counterparts of the psychologist's division of men into extraverts and introverts.

Taking Coleridge's description of the types as a test, I believe we may pretty safely say that of the writers we have so far considered Mr Greene and Mrs Woolf fall into the group represented by Milton: they are introverts: they attract forms and things into the unity of their own ideals. George Eliot, I would say, is certainly in the Shakespearean group; she is an extravert. The next novelist I want to consider is an out-and-out extravert; on the record of his novels it seems that he can pass into and become any character he wishes to. This quality sets him somewhat apart from most contemporary writing, which is largely introverted, and places him more surely than most living English novelists in the main stream of English fiction, which, compared with the French, say, is an extravert tradition. The writer in question is Mr Joyce Cary, and the novel I want to discuss is *The Horse's Mouth*.

In its method this novel, like others of Mr Cary's, takes us straight back to the beginning of the novel in England; straight back to Defoe, the author of the one novel which almost everybody who can read at all has read: *Robinson Crusoe*. You will remember that in *Crusoe* Defoe writes in the first person, as though he himself were the sailor who had been cast away on a desert island, and so successful is he in the illusion he creates that while reading the book we scarcely ever stop to wonder what kind of man the author, Defoe, himself is, what his own opinions are, and so on. *Robinson Crusoe* was not Defoe's only novel, but in his others he follows the same method; he's a pickpocket in *Moll Flanders*, a prostitute in *Roxana*, an adventurer in *Captain Singleton*; and in all these we never think of referring to Defoe himself. Reading Mr Graham Greene, Mrs Woolf and Mr Kingsley Amis, we do not for a moment escape their presence, so individual, idiosyncratic, is the selection of their material and their way of looking at it. One reads Mr Cary, as one does Defoe, almost without reference to the author. One remembers what Keats said of the poet's individuality—he meant the kind of poet he was himself: 'The poet has none, no identity.' Mr Cary as a novelist is, as Coleridge called Shakespeare, a Proteus, that figure in Greek mythology who could turn himself at will into any shape he chose.

Let us look at the opening paragraphs of *The Horse's Mouth*:

> I was walking by the Thames. Half-past morning on an autumn day. Sun in a mist. Like an orange in a fried-fish shop. All bright below. Low tide, dusty water and a crooked bar of straw, chicken-boxes, dirt and oil from mud to mud. Like a viper swimming in skim milk. The old serpent, symbol of nature and love

Five windows light the caverned man; through one he breathes the air
Through one hears music of the spheres; through one can look
And see small portions of the eternal world.

Such as Thames mud turned into a bank of nine carat gold rough from the fire. They say a chap just out of prison runs into the nearest cover; into some dark little room. Like a rabbit put up by a stoat. The sky feels too big for him. But I liked it. I swam in it. I couldn't take my eyes off the clouds, the water, the mud. And I must have been hopping up and down Greenbank Hard for half an hour grinning like a gargoyle, until the wind began to get up my trousers and down my back, and to bring me to myself, as they say. Meaning my liver and lights.

And I perceived that I hadn't time to waste on pleasure. A man of my age has to get on with the job.

I had two and six left from my prison money. I reckoned that five pounds would set me up with bed, board and working capital. That left four pounds seventeen and six to be won. From friends. But when I went over my friends, I seemed to owe them more than that; more than they could afford.

The sun had crackled into flames at the top; the mist was getting thin in places, you could see crooked lines of grey, like old cracks under spring ice. Tide on the turn. Snake broken up. Emeralds and sapphires. Water like bits of gold leaf floating thick and heavy. Gold is the metal of intellect. And all at once, the sun burned through in a new place, at the side, and shot out a ray that hit the Eagle and Child, next the motor-boat factory, right on the new signboard.

Who is this old reprobate just out of prison, walking through East London with no money, debts, the habit of quoting from William Blake's prophetic books, the ability to express himself with such racy exuberance, and with so extraordinary a visual sense? What is the nature of the work he is so eager to get on with? He is obviously a 'character', obviously a man for whom the visible world exists in an almost overpowering intensity. He is in fact Gully Jimson, a painter of genius, and it is the measure of Mr Cary's achievement that he gets completely inside Gully and convinces us to the full of his genius as a wild visionary painter who lives wholly for his painting, is asocial if not anti-social, and, though always stricken with poverty and hatching out ingenious and usually near-criminal schemes for obtaining money, yet retains his integrity as an artist. But besides being a master of paint, Gully is in his own way a master of language, and he expresses himself in an idiom unlike that of any other character in fiction. His idiom is wildly extravagant, colourful, slangy, a completely individual speech. At times his adventures—though we must remember it is Gully himself, not a stickler for facts, who is narrating them—are ludicrous to the point of farce; the occupation of the millionaire's flat, for instance. Yet, somehow, the wild humour does not make for unreality. It makes, instead, for exhilaration, for admiration of Gully's resource and integrity.

Through Gully Jimson Mr Cary creates a whole world. It is an eccentric world, but an authentic image of the real world, for all that. Gully derives much of his power and his vitality, his truth, from Mr Cary's having placed him in the centre of the English tradition of radical nonconformity. It isn't by accident that his favourite poet and painter, the man he always identifies himself with, is Blake: he is part and parcel of the same English tradition as Blake. In a way, indeed, such is the novelist's skill that he appears at times as a modern Blake. His friends, Mr Plant the philosopher, and Ollier the postman, are also English eccentrics, nonconformists, members of tiny societies which gather together to discuss the universe. They are, if you like, cranks; but so were such great English figures as William Fox, Bunyan, Blake himself, Robert Owen, William Morris, Keir Hardie. And what is to be noted, I think, is that though the reader may see in Gully the eternal type of the irresponsible artist, i.e. the artist who decides that art itself is quite big enough for a man to live for, without acquiring other loyalties, to Mr Plant and his friends he is, so to speak, perfectly normal, for they know that religion takes men in diverse ways and painting is as natural and proper a form of religious expression as any other.

So, in *The Horse's Mouth*, Mr Cary has not only succeeded in the extremely difficult task of creating a visionary painter of genius and allowing him to speak for himself, to give us his opinions on almost every conceivable subject, but he uses him also in order to express, from an unusual angle, a vision of the

English nonconformist tradition. In doing so, it seems to me that Mr Cary re-asserts one of the most important qualities of the English spirit.

But Cary, as *The Horse's Mouth* shows, is also a writer of the most exuberant comedy. I doubt if there is a funnier book written in recent years. Cary has the true comic-writer's gift of piling invention upon invention. The novel moves with the speed and gusto—and gusto is the rarest quality in contemporary fiction—of eighteenth-century novelists like Fielding and Smollett, to whose traditions Cary largely returns. For Jimson is really the rogue-hero, looking for a fine wall to paint on as eighteenth-century rogue-heroes looked for a wealthy woman to gull. It is fitting that the novel should rise to a furious crescendo of excitement with Jimson and his young disciples painting a wall in a building which the local authorities are busily demolishing as unsafe.

VI. A Woman of the Pharisees
François Mauriac

Publishers find an apparently unconquerable aversion among English readers towards Continental fiction, and it is for this reason that I have chosen a French novel as my sixth specimen of contemporary fiction. For this aversion is surely stupid and irrational. It is not even provincial, it is parochial, the fruit of intellectual isolationism. It is through its art and in particular its literature that we can most fully know and understand another people. Travel helps, of course, but few of us travel often enough or stay long enough in a country; few of us make intimate friends with even one Frenchman as a result of our fortnight's annual visit to Paris. It is scarcely possible. But French fiction is as nearly accessible to us as our own, and the French novelist, like his English colleague, is a man speaking to men, and no matter how 'French' he may be, if he is a good novelist, he is only incidentally a Frenchman.

Nor need the language barrier be of any real importance; the great French novels have all been translated, and so have many of the best contemporary French novels, for the most part, excellently. The stumbling blocks, the factors that make for a sense of foreignness, are really very trivial; little more generally than different habits of eating, for instance, or the unfamiliarity arising from a different educational system. And when we do come across evidences of what seem to us foreignness, qualities, ways of behaviour and thought that we feel we would not find in an English writer, surely it is exactly here that the value of the French novel is most obvious. The context of the novel offers us a chance to understand and appreciate that foreignness. Even so, the unfamiliarity of the scene, the unusualness of the characters' thought and behaviour, is often no greater than the English reader finds in, say, American or even Irish and Welsh fiction; and yet he does not refuse to read the novels of Mr Hemingway and Mr Steinbeck, Mr Liam O'Flaherty and Mr Seán O'Fáoláin, Mr Rhys Davies and Mr Richard Llewellyn.

The only way to conquer an aversion towards European fiction is to read it.

But there is one broad distinction worth stating between the typical English and the typical French novel. That is in the novelists' approach to their characters. The very word character helps in stating the distinction, for in English it is an ambiguous word. It can mean, simply, an imaginary person invented by a novelist; but it may also mean a person distinguished by odd behaviour, an eccentric. We say in real life of a man of strongly marked idiosyncrasy that he is a 'character'. It is a fact that English novelists have always tended to see their imaginary persons as eccentric persons; the two meanings have tended to overlap. Look at the novels we have been discussing. George Eliot sees some of her characters as 'characters', Mr Brooke, for instance, in *Middlemarch.* Virginia Woolf's Mrs Swithin is, I think, a 'character'. And there can be no doubt that Mr Cary's Gully Jimson is a glorious 'character'. French novelists practically never see their characters as 'characters'. It points, no doubt, to a difference in the psychologies of the two peoples; it means that a French Dickens, whose works are a positive National Gallery of 'characters', is almost inconceivable. You might put the difference between the English and French ways of expressing character like this: the English novelist tends to work from the highly individual, the highly idiosyncratic, to the general type the Frenchman tends to work from the general type to the individual. It was a great, and very French, novelist who declared: 'Art is not made to paint the exceptions . . .' adding that the characters most suited to fiction were the 'more general' because they were the more typical. So if a French novelist invents a miser or a hypocrite what interests him, what he stresses, is the quality of miserliness or of hypocrisy. An English novelist would be more likely to stress the comic aspects of miserliness or hypocrisy, to such an extent, perhaps, that both he and the reader would be in danger of forgetting the vice in their appreciation of the idiosyncrasies that were its result. Perhaps this is another way of saying, though like all generalizations it is an over-simplification, that English novelists tend to write as humorists whereas French novelists tend to write as psychologists.

But let us turn to the French novel I have chosen as my example. It is *A Woman of the Pharisees*, by M. François Mauriac, in Mr Gerard Hopkins's beautiful translation. The title will give a clue to the nature of the novel, to M. Mauriac's aim in writing it. For what were the qualities which especially distinguished the Pharisees? Primarily, an over-insistence on the letter of the religious law at the expense of the spirit of the law, and then, as a result of this, self-righteousness, a 'holier-than-thou' attitude. Christ—I quote from Peake's *Commentary on the Bible*—accused the Pharisees of 'hypocrisy, of self-satisfaction and display, of love of honours and lack of humility. . . . He denounced their casuistry, and the wants of a sense of proportion which made them treat niceties of legal observance as of equal importance with its weightier matters. Perhaps the most serious charge of all lies in the assertion that they were blind leaders, who kept men out of the Kingdom while refusing to enter themselves. . . . The denunciations of the Pharisees were prompted by compassion for the people they misled'.

Now you will not have to read many pages of *A Woman of*

the Pharisees before you realize that M. Mauriac is a man of religion, a novelist whose theme is the relation of man to God, for whom the only reality is man's relation to God. And it soon becomes apparent that in Brigitte Pian he is describing a Pharisee in the strict, not the merely abusive, sense. She is a woman, he tells us, 'sincerely anxious to do good' in every circumstance of her life; but she wears an 'armour of perfection':

There had been a time when she was worried by the spiritual aridity which marked her relations with her God: but since then she had read somewhere that it is as a rule the beginners on whom the tangible marks of Grace are showered, since it is only in that way that they can be extricated from the slough of this world and set upon the right path. The kind of insensitiveness which afflicted her was, she gathered, a sign that she had long ago emerged from those lower regions of the spiritual life where fervour is usually suspect. In this way her frigid soul was led on to glory in its own lack of warmth. It did not occur to her that never, for a single moment, even in the earliest stages of her search for perfection, had she felt any emotion which could be said to have borne the faintest resemblance to love: that she had never approached her Master save with the object of calling His attention to her own remarkably rapid progress along the Way, and suggesting that He give special heed to her singular merits.

She is a woman of inordinate spiritual ambition who is completely lacking in charity in the theological sense. And the spiritual damage she does is incalculable. She perverts, in some cases ruins, the lives of all those who come into intimate contact with her. M. Mauriac's exposure of her is complete and remorseless; it is an exhaustive psychological study of a pious woman in whom righteousness has become self-righteousness, who has deluded herself into believing her lust for power over others is a concern for their spiritual salvation. But what is more remarkable is M. Mauriac's attitude to her. Her creator sees her always in the light of Christian charity, of compassion. It is here, I think, that one sees the difference between the French attitude to character and the English. It would be scarcely possible for an English novelist to have made her other than a hypocrite or a moral monster. But what interests M. Mauriac is the nature of pharisaism itself.

The problem as stated by M. Mauriac is, it may be admitted, not one that could be easily reproduced in English terms, in an English setting. By this I do not, of course, mean that the Pharisee is unknown in England; simply that M. Mauriac examines it in terms of a Christian, Catholic community of a kind that scarcely exists in this country. I do not think that this need in the least diminish the value of the novel for English readers. Indeed, the very fact that a universal problem is examined from a position remote from the reader's own may result in its being lit with a more intense and powerful illumination than would otherwise be possible. I believe that this is so with M. Mauriac's novel. One does not have to be one of the author's fellow-religionists to appreciate it. I can imagine no sensitive, willing reader, whatever his religious belief or lack of belief, who would not find himself disturbed by *A Woman of the Pharisees*, disturbed in the best sense, or find his knowledge of the motives of human action deeper and his human sympathies extended as a result of reading it. And that, after all, is the great end of the novel as a literary form: to extend our range of human sympathies.

VII. LUCKY JIM
KINGSLEY AMIS

THERE IS nothing so rare as the good comic novel, the novel in the classic tradition of comedy; and there is nothing, when it does arrive, more disconcerting. Kingsley Amis's *Lucky Jim* is a novel in the classic tradition of comedy. But what does that mean? We see the classic tradition of comedy at its purest in English fiction in the novels of Fielding, Jane Austen and George Meredith. These writers were moralists and for them comedy was a weapon in the service of right behaviour, one might almost say good manners. They correct follies—self-delusions, affectations, pride, pretentiousness, sentimentality, self-indulgence of whatever kind—by making them ridiculous. So fundamental to the novels of all these writers, is a set of values, the notion of a norm of right thinking and right behaviour. It is this that gives their moral judgments weight, as it is in the departure from the norm that their characters are shown as ridiculous.

To understand comedy, then, it is necessary to understand the novelist's values, to gauge his notion of the normal. On the surface, *Lucky Jim* is conventional enough: it is the story of a young man's entry into the world. But there the resemblance with the ordinary novel on the theme ends. Jim Dixon, we discover, is not at all the sensitive young man experience leads us to expect to find in such novels. His general attitude to his surroundings is one of disgust, not of aesthetic disgust but of something much more closely akin to moral disgust, disgust at pretentiousness, at cultural cant. He is a lecturer in history at a provincial university, when the book opens very much concerned that his year of probation is coming to an end and, since his career thus far has been anything but auspicious, that his contract may be renewed. Perhaps it is significant that he speaks with a Northern accent and that he is a graduate not of one of the ancient universities but of Leicester. He is not at all posh; he lacks savoir-faire; he is indeed singularly graceless, and by a paradox his gracelessness is his saving grace. What he does have is an angry impatience of the bogus, and in his life as a university lecturer he finds himself enmeshed in the bogus. There is the bogus, self-conscious culture of Professor Welch, with his arty parties, his musical evenings complete with recorders and folk songs and rounds and catches, and with his painter son for whom the practice of art is a convenient excuse for selfishness and self-seeking. There is the bogus personal relationship offered Jim by his neurotic colleague Margaret, a parasite on his pity for her and who, as it were, woos him by emotional blackmail. And then there is what seems to him the whole bogus externals of his job, what may be called the academic racket.

As we meet him first, Jim is doing his best to compromise, to play the racket as enthusiastically as he can, for his livelihood is at stake and his career has begun disastrously, with what can only appear to everyone else as a gratuitous physical assault on the Professor of English. He has much to live down, and if he is to succeed he must suck up. Alas, his reluctant integrity gets in the way. With the best will in the world, he cannot avoid doing the wrong thing. And therein lies his luck. His tactlessnesses, his gaucheries, his crude sense of humour are in fact signs of his integrity. He goes to his Professor's for the week-end and, drunk, burns the bed clothes with a forgotten cigarette—and his efforts to hide and destroy the evidence of this accident make what is probably the funniest passage in any English novel since Evelyn Waugh wrote *Decline and Fall.* His final chance to rehabilitate himself is no less disastrous. He has to give a public lecture before the University and the local dignitaries on the subject of Merrie England, a subject dear to his Professor. Nervous and having drunk too much sherry at the cocktail party before, but still anxious to conform, he finds to his horror as he begins to speak that he is parodying the manner first of his Professor and then of the Principal of the University; but before he passes out he manages to deliver his final peroration. It is not, however, the peroration he had planned. That was to run:

'What, finally, is the practical application of all this? Can anything be done to halt, or even to hinder, the processes I have described? I say to you that something can be done by each one of us here tonight. Each of us can resolve to do something, every day, to resist the application of manufactured standards, to protest against ugly articles of furniture and table-ware, to speak out against sham architecture, to resist the importation into more and more public places of loudspeakers relaying the Light Programme, to say one word against the Yellow Press, against the best-seller, against the theatre organ, to say one word for the instinctive culture of the integrated village-type community. In that way, we shall be saying a word, however small in its individual effect, for our native tradition, for our common heritage, in short, for what we once had and may, some day, have again—Merrie England.'

It becomes, instead:

'What, finally, is the practical application of all this?' Dixon said in his normal voice. He felt he was in the grip of some vertigo, hearing himself talking without consciously willing any words. 'Listen and I'll tell you. The point about Merrie England is that it was about the most un-Merrie period in our history. It's only the home-made pottery crowd, the organic husbandry crowd, the recorder-playing crowd, the Esperanto. . . .' He paused and swayed; the heat, the drink, the nervousness, the guilt, joined forces in him. . . . Chairs scraped on either side of him; a hand caught at his shoulder and made him stumble. With Welch's arm round his shoulders he sank to his knees, half-hearing the Principal's voice saying above a tumult: ' . . . from finishing his lecture through sudden indisposition. I'm sure you'll all. . . .'

I've done it now, he managed to think.

If the novel ends happily, with Jim triumphant, escaped from the bogus and on the verge of a new life with a new girl, that too is in the tradition of classical comedy, which leaves discomforted those that need the correcting touch of ridicule and the hero unscathed, albeit the wiser. Kingsley Amis might have made Jim a *naif*, a Chaplinesque figure of innocence. He does not. Instead, Jim Dixon emerges as what Wyndham Lewis would call a 'soldier of humour': it is he who attacks the pretensions of his enemies, even though there are times when he can do so only in secret and by pulling the funny faces that seem appropriate to the situation.

The point of view informing *Lucky Jim* is reminiscent of that of George Orwell. Orwell was not a comic novelist; but he had a sure perception of the truth about the state of England and a deep distrust of the fashionable in culture and the arts. He cut through the nonsense. And this is what Kingsley Amis does in *Lucky Jim*. Throughout the novel, at the root of its comedy, is an implied contrast between the pretensions with which the Welches, father and son, invest themselves and the actual situation in post-war, welfare-state England. That is one great merit of the novel. The other, of course, is the way in which it is executed, the comic invention. Kingsley Amis, one feels, has put himself to school with the great eighteenth-century comic novelists, Fielding and Smollett. This means that his approach to his characters and theme is tough, virile, direct and full of gusto. *Lucky Jim* is masculine work, and to have brought back some of the vigour of eighteenth-century comedy into the English novel at a time when it often seems in danger of becoming soft with excessive sensibility is part of Kingsley Amis's achievement.

[illegible] ... on the other side of him, a hand clutched at his elbow ... the summoning. With Welch's arm round his shoulders, he ... his knees, half-hearing the Principal's voice saying above: '... from finishing his lecture through sudden indisposition. I'm sure you'll all ...'

He's done it now, he managed to think.

If the novel ends happily, with Jim triumphantly escaped from the bogus and on the verge of a new life with a new girl, that too is in the tradition of classical comedy, which leaves discomforted those that need the correcting touch of ridicule and the hero unscathed, albeit the wiser. Kingsley Amis might have made Jim a *naïf*, a simple-minded figure of innocence. He does not. Instead, Jim Dixon emerges as what Wyndham Lewis would call a 'soldier of humour'; it is he who attacks the pretensions of his enemies, even though there are times when he can do so only in secret and by pulling the funny faces that seem appropriate to the situation.

The point of view that informs *Lucky Jim* is reminiscent of that of George Orwell. Orwell was not a comic novelist, but he had a sure perception of the realities of the state of England and a deep distrust of the pretentious in culture and the arts. He cut through the nonsense, and this is what Kingsley Amis does in *Lucky Jim*. Throughout the novel, at the root of its comedy, is an implicit contrast between the pretensions with which the Welches, father and son, invest themselves and the actual situation in post-war, welfare-state England. That is one great merit of the novel. The other, of course, is the way in which it is executed, the comic invention. Kingsley Amis, rightly, has put himself to school with the great eighteenth-century comic novelists, Fielding and Smollett. This means that his approach to his characters and theme is tough, virile, direct and full of gusto. *Lucky Jim* is masculine work, and to have brought back some of the vigour of eighteenth-century comedy into the English novel at a time when it often seems in danger of becoming soft with excessive sensibility is part of Kingsley Amis's achievement.